TOP 20 ESL WORD GAMES

BEGINNING VOCABULARY DEVELOPMENT

MARJORIE FUCHS

BERENICE PLISKIN

CLAUDIA KARABAIC SARGENT

Longman

New York

Top 20 ESL Word Games

Longman, 10 Bank Street, White Plains, N.Y. 10606

Associated companies:
Longman Group Ltd., London
Longman Cheshire Pty., Melbourne
Longman Paul Pty., Auckland
Copp Clark Pitman, Toronto

Distributed in the United Kingdom by Longman Group
Ltd., Longman House, Burnt Mill, Harlow, Essex CM20
2JE, England and by associated companies, branches,
and representatives throughout the world.

Executive editor: Joanne Dresner
Development editor: Nancy Perry
Production editor: Helen B. Ambrosio
Text design adaptation: The Quarasan Group, Inc.
Cover illustration and design: Claudia Karabaic Sargent
Text art: Claudia Karabaic Sargent, Pencil Point Studio
Production supervisor: Kathleen M. Ryan

ISBN: 0–8013–0365–6

3 4 5 6 7 8 9 10-HC-95949392

CONTENTS

About the Puzzles

Top 20 ESL Word Games helps students learn basic vocabulary through stimulating and instructive games and puzzles. Students learn and practice vocabulary relating to everyday topics, such as food, family, clothes, time, transportation, sports and electronic equipment. New vocabulary is recycled in later units. At the same time students are practicing vocabulary, they are also reinforcing their knowledge of grammatical points, such as subject pronouns, possessive nouns and adjectives, definite and indefinite articles, prepositional phrases, irregular verbs and the formation of negative and interrogative sentences. Activities also provide practice in life skills, such as telling time, reading train schedules and ordering in a restaurant. In addition, students are exposed to various written forms, such as postcards, letters, calendars, schedules and menus. The recurring section "What About You?" gives students the opportunity to personalize what they have learned by writing and talking about themselves.

The puzzles and activities have been designed to appeal to the needs and interests of beginning students of all ages—from teenagers to young adults. In Unit 1, the students meet a group of rock musicians, Rosie and the Firefighters. Throughout the book they follow the activities of the group, which reflect the students' own lives and interests.

Blackline Masters

These blackline masters aid instruction in a variety of ways:
- They are easily reproducible.
- They can be used as enrichment for the more advanced students or reinforcement for the students who need more practice on a particular skill.
- They provide valuable motivation in the form of high-interest activities.

- They provide a change of pace and can be used for self-study, pair or small group work.
- They offer opportunities for self-correction for the whole class.
- They offer the teacher a ready-made and efficient way to assess the needs of the class on each topic.

How to Use the Puzzles

Each unit presents several puzzles and activities that students can work on independently, in pairs or in small groups. Pair and group work are especially beneficial in practicing oral/aural skills. Because each unit develops a specific topic, you can use the activities to introduce a topic or as reinforcement after a topic has been taught. The Table of Contents lists the topic or topics of each unit. A short warm-up activity can motivate students and help with pronunciation.

The last page of each unit (except for Unit 20, which is a review unit presenting no new vocabulary) has a section called "Do You Know These Words?" This provides the students with an alphabetized list, organized by part of speech, of the key vocabulary items from the unit. This list can be used to help the students do the activities and can also serve as a summary for future study. Throughout the book you will see this symbol next to certain activities: 📖 These activities are intended to be done with the help of either the vocabulary list or a bilingual dictionary.

Encourage students to work together and pool their knowledge. Then with the whole class you can check students' work and reinforce the vocabulary and structures of the unit. Above all, use *Top 20 ESL Word Games* to create a relaxed and enjoyable environment to learn and practice vocabulary and promote conversation. Have fun!

1 Meet and Greet the Stars

Hello, my name is Rosie. I am a *singer* and I *play the guitar.*
Hi, my name is Artie. I play the *drums.*
My name is Johnny. I play the *saxophone.*
We are *rock musicians.* We travel and give *concerts.*
The name of our *group* is Rosie and the Firefighters.

Write *True* or *False*. Correct the statements that are false.

1. Her name is <u>Jane</u>.
   _____*False. Her name is Rosie.*_____

2. She is a <u>singer</u>.
   _____

3. She plays the <u>drums</u>.
   _____

4. Johnny plays the <u>guitar</u>.
   _____

5. There are <u>five</u> drums.
   _____

6. Artie plays the <u>saxophone</u>.
   _____

7. They are <u>rock musicians</u>.
   _____

2 What About You?

1. ROSIE: My name is Rosie. What is your name?

   YOU: _____

2. ROSIE: I like rock *music.* Do you like music? What kind? (rock, *jazz, classical music,* . . .)

   YOU: _____

3. ROSIE: I play the guitar. Do you play a *musical instrument*? What kind?

   YOU: _____

4. ROSIE: My favorite singer is Julio Iglesias. My favorite group is U2. What is the name of your favorite singer or group?

   YOU: _____

3 Mix and Match

Match the questions and answers.

	A		B
_e_	1. What is his name?		a. Yes, very much.
____	2. Does he like music?		b. The saxophone.
____	3. What kind of music does he like?		c. Rock.
____	4. What is his favorite instrument?		d. No, he doesn't.
____	5. Does he sing?		e. Johnny.

4 Tune Up

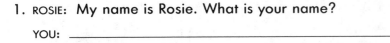

Write the word for each picture in the puzzle.

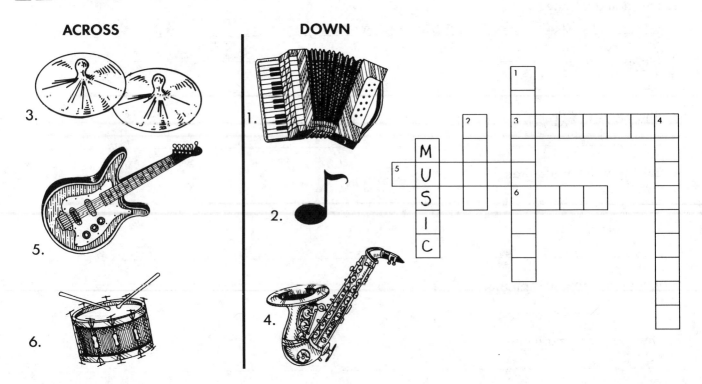

ACROSS

3.

5.

6.

DOWN

1.

2.

4.

5 A Letter from Rosie

Complete the letter from Rosie.

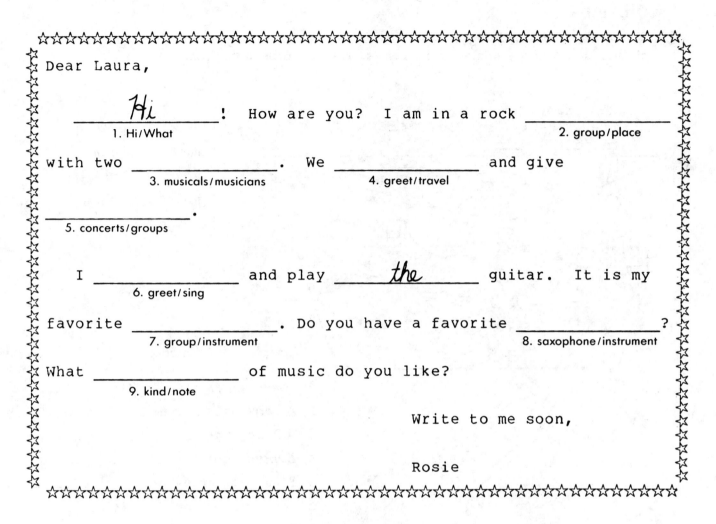

Dear Laura,

_____*Hi*_____! How are you? I am in a rock _____
1. Hi/What   2. group/place

with two _____. We _____ and give
        3. musicals/musicians   4. greet/travel

_____.
5. concerts/groups

I _____ and play ____*the*____ guitar. It is my
     6. greet/sing

favorite _____. Do you have a favorite _____?
        7. group/instrument   8. saxophone/instrument

What _____ of music do you like?
     9. kind/note

Write to me soon,

Rosie

Do You Know These Words?

Nouns	Verbs	Adjective	Expression
accordion	give	favorite	What kind?
classical music	greet		
concert	like		
cymbal	meet		
drum	play		
group	sing		
guitar	travel		
jazz			
music			
musical instrument			
name			
note			
rock musician			
saxophone			
singer			
star			

1 Colorama

Johnny likes **fruits** and **vegetables**. He also likes his cats, Maggie and Kate. Look at the pictures and write the names of the **colors**. Use the words in the box.

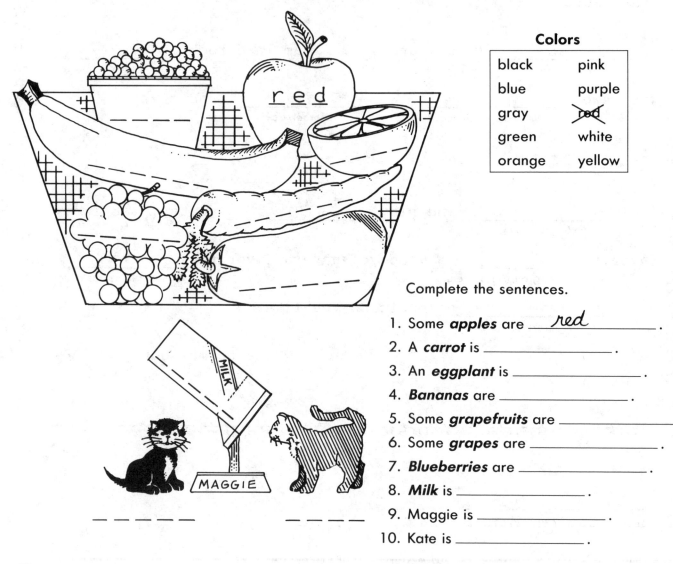

Colors

black	pink
blue	purple
gray	~~red~~
green	white
orange	yellow

r e d

Complete the sentences.

1. Some **apples** are _____red_____ .
2. A **carrot** is _____ .
3. An **eggplant** is _____ .
4. **Bananas** are _____ .
5. Some **grapefruits** are _____ .
6. Some **grapes** are _____ .
7. **Blueberries** are _____ .
8. **Milk** is _____ .
9. Maggie is _____ .
10. Kate is _____ .

MAGGIE

_ _ _ _ _   _ _ _ _ _

2 Splash!

Look at this palette. Unscramble the colors. Make new colors.
   1. **red** + **yellow** = **orange**

1. ERD + LOLEWY = O R A N G E

2. LUBE + DER = _ _ _ _ _ _

3. UBEL + LLEYOW = _ _ _ _ _

4. TWIHE + DRE = _ _ _ _

5. THEIW + LABKC = _ _ _ _

3 The Rhyming Room

📖 Look at this room. The things in the room rhyme with the names of colors. For example, the **light** is **white,** and the **backpack** is **black**. What are the colors of the other things in the room?

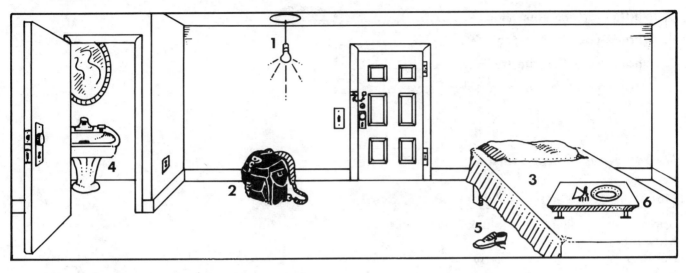

1. _The light is white._
2. _The backpack is black._
3. _____
4. _____
5. _____
6. _____

4 Picture Puzzle

📖 Look at Artie's **striped** sweater. There are three colors in it. What are they? Solve the picture puzzle and find out.

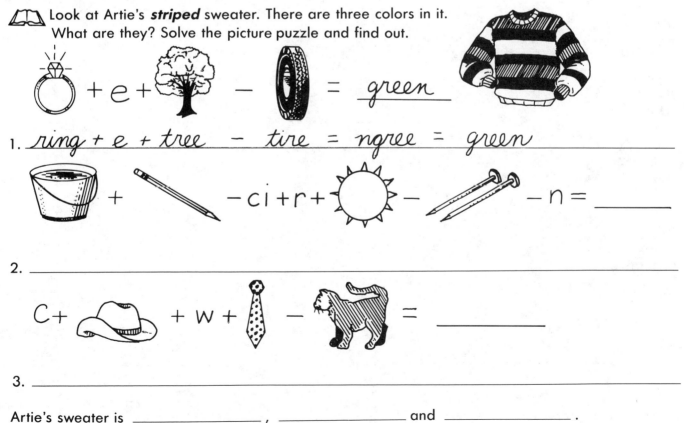

1. _ring + e + tree − tire = ngree = green_
2. _____
3. _____

Artie's sweater is _____ , _____ and _____ .

5 What About You?

1. What color are your eyes? _____

2. What color is your pen? _____

3. What color are your shoes? _____

4. What is your favorite color? _____

5. What is your favorite fruit? _____

6. What is your favorite vegetable? _____

_____

Do You Know These Words?

Nouns	Verb	Adjectives	Adverb
apple	like	black	also
backpack		blue	
banana		gray	
bed		green	
blueberries		orange	
carrot		pink	
cat		purple	
color		red	
eggplant		striped	
eyes		white	
fruit		yellow	
grapefruit			
grapes			
hat			
light			
milk			
nail			
pail			
palette			
pen			
pencil			
ring			
shoe			
sink			
sun			
tie			
tire			
tray			
tree			
vegetable			

1 Family Portrait

Fold this page back along the fold line (fold ⟷). Follow the directions for Part 1.

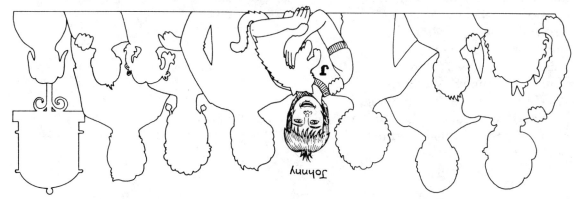

Part 2: Write the names of Johnny's *relatives.* Do not look at the picture in Part 1!

⟵——————→ FOLD ⟵——————→ FOLD ⟵——————→ FOLD⟵

Part 1: This is Johnny's family. Study the picture for two minutes.

Now turn the page over to Part 2. Follow the directions for Part 2.

2 Family Find

There are 12 family words in this box. The words go ⟶, ⟵, ↑, ↓, and ↘. Can you find them?

```
S A G R A N D M O T H E R
I O B H L M E R T N O F E
S A B F B C C L A U M R T
T E E A G B O O C A T D H
E M O T H E R O U S Q M G
R L R H Y P G O D S L E L
A O M E L C N U T R I L B
R O D R I B A G B H O N D
O G R A N D F A T H E R Y
N J A M L E D T O O M R S
```

1. *grandmother*
2. _____
3. _____
4. _____
5. _____
6. _____
7. _____
8. _____
9. _____
10. _____
11. _____
12. _____

3 Family Match

Read about Johnny's family. Then match the names in Column A with Johnny's relatives in Column B. You will use one answer more than one time.

Rick is the **husband** of Johnny's mother.
Susan is the sister of Johnny's brother.
Mark is the **son** of Johnny's father.
Sam is the husband of Johnny's aunt.
Linda is the sister of Johnny's father.
Louis is the father of Johnny's mother.
Annie is the **wife** of Johnny's grandfather.
Sharon is the **daughter** of Johnny's grandmother and grandfather.
Stuart is the son of Johnny's aunt and uncle.
Phyllis is Stuart's sister.

	A		B
_g_	1. Rick	a.	mother
____	2. Susan	b.	uncle
____	3. Mark	c.	sister
____	4. Sam	d.	grandfather
____	5. Linda IS JOHNNY'S	e.	aunt
____	6. Louis	f.	grandmother
____	7. Annie	g.	father
____	8. Sharon	h.	cousin
____	9. Stuart	i.	brother
____	10. Phyllis		

4 What About You?

Complete your family chart.

Relative	Name(s)	Relative	Name(s)
mother	_____	son	_____
father	_____	daughter	_____
sister	_____	aunt	_____
brother	_____	uncle	_____
husband / wife	_____	cousin	_____

Do You Know These Words?

Nouns

aunt	dog	mother
bird	family	relative
brother	father	sister
cat	grandfather	son
cousin	grandmother	uncle
daughter	husband	wife

UNIT 4

1 Where Are They?

Look at the picture of Johnny's house.

Now complete the sentences. Use the words in the box.

garage	bedroom
dining room	tree
living room	~~garden~~
bathroom	kitchen

1. Johnny's grandmother is in the _____garden_____.

2. Johnny's dog is in the _____.

3. Johnny's father and uncle are in the _____.

4. Johnny's sister and cousin Phyllis are in the _____.

5. Johnny's brother and cousin Stuart are in the _____.

6. Johnny's mother and aunt are in the _____.

7. Johnny's cat is in the _____.

8. Johnny's grandfather is in the _____.

9. Johnny's bird is in the _____.

2 True or False?

Write **True** or **False**. Correct the statements that are false.

1. Johnny's cousin Phyllis is on the <u>kitchen</u> floor.

   False. Phyllis is on the bedroom floor.

2. His sister is on the <u>bed</u>.

   _____

3. The <u>dog</u> is on the bathtub.

   _____

4. There is fruit on the table in the <u>dining room</u>.

   _____

5. The refrigerator is <u>gray</u>.

   _____

6. There is a couch in the <u>garage</u>.

   _____

7. There are <u>bicycles</u> in the garage.

   _____

3 Secret Code

This is a note to Johnny from his brother Mark. A number = a letter. Can you read the note?
Remember: This is a note to Johnny from Mark!

EXAMPLE: A=2, H=3, J=7

H J H 3 4 7 9 3 1 1 5,	
A H A 4 2 8 4 1 6 3 10 13 2 11 14 10 1.	
A 8 2 11 12	

Where is Mark? _____

_____?

Do You Know These Words?

Nouns

bathroom	chair	garage	refrigerator
bathtub	couch	garden	table
bed	dining room	house	toilet
bedroom	floor	kitchen	tree
bicycle (bike)	flower	living room	

1 Late for a Concert

Rosie is late. She is giving a rock concert at 10:00 P.M. Look at Rosie's **suitcase** and look at her living room. Unscramble the words and write them in the column labeled "Things in Rosie's suitcase."

	Things in Rosie's suitcase	**Things NOT in Rosie's suitcase**
toca	*coat*	*sunglasses*
lobsue		
thisr		
lawelt		
kajcte		
enomy		
kisrt		
stpan		
ehoss		
inurnng ehoss		
stoob		
twesaer		
sresd		

Now look at Rosie's living room again. This was BEFORE Rosie **packed** her suitcase. What is NOT in Rosie's suitcase? Circle the items in the picture. Then write the words in the column labeled "Things **NOT** in Rosie's suitcase."

2 True or False?

📖 Look at the picture on page 11. Write **True** or **False**. Correct the statements that are false.

1. This is <u>Johnny's</u> living room.
   False. This is Rosie's living room.

2. The radio is <u>on the floor.</u>

3. There are <u>two</u> hats in the living room.

4. There is a picture of a <u>saxophone</u> on the record album.

5. There are flowers on Rosie's <u>sweater.</u>

6. Rosie's <u>bathing suit</u> is striped.

7. There is a clock on the <u>table.</u>

3 What Are They?

Look at the picture of Rosie's living room. Complete the information.

1. There are four items with stripes.
   a. *bathing suit*   c. _____
   b. _____   d. _____

2. There are four items with **polka dots.**
   a. *blouse*   c. _____
   b. _____   d. _____

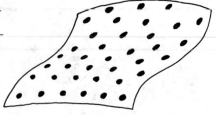

4 Which Word Doesn't Belong?

1. boots   running shoes   ~~skirts~~

2. blouse   bag   sweater

3. radio   stereo   camera

4. sunglasses   wallet   suitcase

5. gloves   boots   pants

5 Blue Shoe Rock

Rosie and the Firefighters sing this song. Complete it with the words in the box. Every two lines rhyme. For example, *two* rhymes with *you*.

~~blue~~	hat
cat	love
chair	rock
clock	shoe
do	there
glove	you

I like the color ___blue___ .
            1

What about _____ ?
     2

I look at my bedroom _____ .
         3

It's OK, but you're not _____ .
      4

I look at my bedroom _____ .
      5

And sing my favorite music— _____ .
       6

Your coat, your boots, your big white _____ .
         7

Your bird, your dog, and Kate, your _____ .
        8

I like my belt and _____ .
     9

But it's you I really _____ .
      10

I like my big blue _____ .
     11

But I love you. Yes, I _____ .
     12

Do You Know These Words?

Nouns

bag	cap	hat	radio	skirt	table
bathing suit	clock	jacket	record	sock	wall
belt	coat	money	record album	stereo	wallet
blouse	dress	pants	running shoe	suitcase	
boot	glove	picture	shirt	sunglasses	
camera	(hand)bag	polka dots	shoe	sweater	

Verb
pack

Expression
in a rush

1 Name the Day

Do you know the **days** of the **week**? Unscramble the words. Then write the days in the boxes. Write the TIME YOU START and the TIME YOU FINISH. How fast are you?

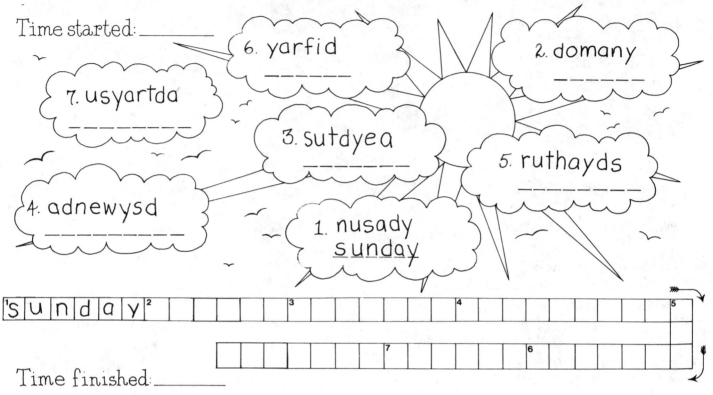

Time started: _____

6. yarfid
_____

2. domany
_____

7. usyartda
_____

3. sutdyea
_____

5. ruthayds
_____

4. adnewysd
_____

1. nusady
sunday

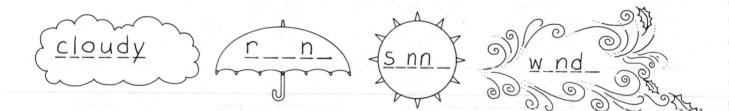

| ¹s | u | n | d | a | y² | | | | ³ | | | | | | | ⁴ | | | | | | | | ⁵ |

| | | | | | | | | ⁷ | | | | | | ⁶ | | | | | | |

Time finished: _____

2 Weather Watch

Fill in the blanks with A, E, I, O, U, and Y. Then complete the seven-day **weather forecast.**

c l o u d y

r _ _ n _

s _ nn _

w _ nd _

1	2	3	4	5	6	7
Sunday						
(cloud)	(umbrella)	(wind)	(sun)	(sun)	(umbrella)	(umbrella)
cloudy						

3 Artie's Schedule

Look at Artie's *schedule* for the week.

Mon.	Tues.	Wed.	Thurs.	Fri.	Sat.	Sun.
Travel to Chicago (crossed out, sun drawn)	Give concert	Meet Aunt Alice at 5:00	Play sax. with Johnny	Pack	Travel to Detroit. Meet Rick	Give concert at 10:00

Now complete Artie's postcard.

Mon. Aug. 11

Dear Cousin Rick,
  Hi! Today is __Monday__
and I'm in _____ [1] with
Rosie and Johnny. [2] The weather
is _____. _____ (Tuesday)
we give [3] a rock concert [4] at the
Banana Club. On _____ I see
Aunt Alice. Oh, and on _____ [5]
we travel to Detroit! [6]
  See you on _____ [7] and at the
concert on _____ [8]!
  Artie

Rick Castelli
2345 Cumberland
Detroit, Mich.

4 What About You?

1. Today is _____.
2. Tomorrow is _____.
3. My favorite day is _____.
4. I _____ on Mondays.
5. I like _____ weather.

Do You Know These Words?

Days	Nouns	Adjectives
Monday	day	cloudy
Tuesday	forecast	rainy
Wednesday	schedule	sunny
Thursday	today	windy
Friday	tomorrow	
Saturday	weather	
Sunday	week	

1 Name the Month

Write the names of the *months.* Write the TIME YOU START and the TIME YOU FINISH.

Time started: _____

April	August	December	February	January	July
June	March	May	November	October	September

1. _____

2. _____

3. _____

4. _____

5. _____

6. _____

7. _____

8. _____

9. _____

10. _____

11. _____

12. _____

Time finished: _____

2 Season Stumper!

Write the word for each picture. Then unscramble the letters in the circles to spell a *season.*

1.

i c e

Season: ○○○○○○

2.

Season: ○○○○○○

3.

_ _ _ ○

4.

3 Happy Birthday!

Can you guess the month or season?

1. Rosie's **birthday** is in the winter. It isn't in December. It's in J a n u a r y .
2. Johnny's birthday is in the spring. It isn't in April. It's in __ __ __ __ __ .
3. Artie's birthday isn't in the winter or summer. It's in the __ __ __ __ __ __ .
4. Maggie's birthday is in the summer. It isn't in June. It's in __ __ __ __ .
5. Kate's birthday is in __ __ __ . It's in the __ __ __ __ __ __ .

4 What About You?

1. What is your favorite season? _____
2. What month is your birthday? _____

Do You Know These Words?

Months		Seasons	Nouns			Verb
January	July	spring	apple	ice	season	swim
February	August	summer	birthday	ice cream	snow	
March	September	fall	fire	leaf	sun	
April	October	winter	football	month	umbrella	
May	November		grass	plant	water	
June	December		hat	rose	wind	

1 Number Drawing

Write the *numbers* next to the words. Then fill in all the areas in the picture for those numbers.

four ___4___   eighty _____   thirty-five _____   fifteen + ten = _____

thirteen _____   seventy _____   forty-six _____   six × three = _____

eight _____   twenty-one _____   fifty-two _____   twenty ÷ two = _____

ninety _____   nineteen _____   sixty-seven _____   thirty − ten = _____

six × four = _____

2 Sizing Them Up

Put the fish in order from BIGGEST to smallest. Use the words in the box.

| eighth | fifth | ~~first~~ | fourth | ninth |
| second | seventh | sixth | tenth | third |

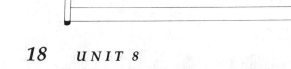

first

3 Rhymes

Complete with numbers.

What number rhymes with. . .?

1. ⓣ w o

2. _ _ O

3. _ _ _ O

4. _ O _ O _

5. _____ O O _

6. O _ _

Now unscramble the letters in the circles. What number is it? __ __ __ __ __ __ __ __

4 What's Next?

Complete the series.

1. one, two, three, *four* _____
2. two, four, six, _____
3. three, six, nine, _____
4. one, three, five, _____
5. thirty, forty, fifty, _____
6. nine, eight, seven, _____
7. two, four, eight, sixteen, _____
8. first, third, fifth, _____

_____
Do You Know These Words?

Cardinal Numbers			Ordinal Numbers	Expression
one	eleven	twenty-one	first	How many?
two	twelve	twenty-two	second	
three	thirteen	thirty	third	
four	fourteen	forty	fourth	
five	fifteen	fifty	fifth	
six	sixteen	sixty	sixth	
seven	seventeen	seventy	seventh	
eight	eighteen	eighty	eighth	
nine	nineteen	ninety	ninth	
ten	twenty	one hundred	tenth	

1 A Clockwise Game

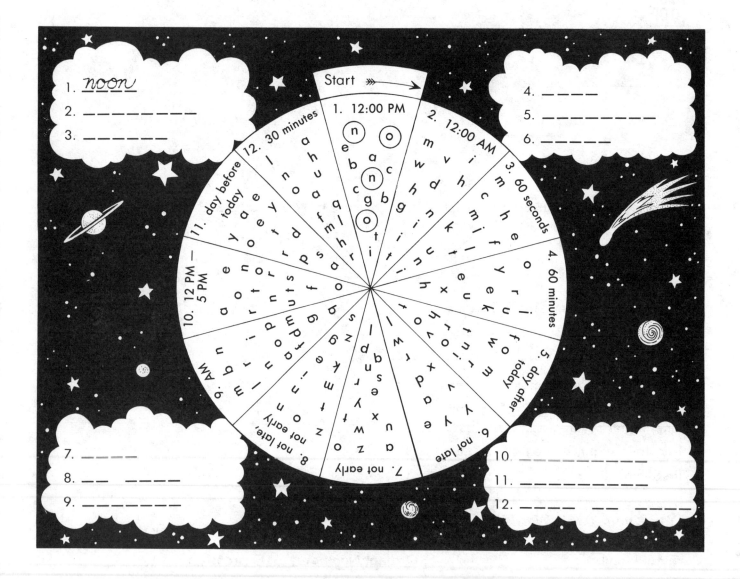 Read the **time** expressions in the circle. Then circle the letters of the word for the time expression. Write the word.

afternoon	early	half an hour	hour	late	midnight
minute	morning	~~noon~~	on time	tomorrow	yesterday

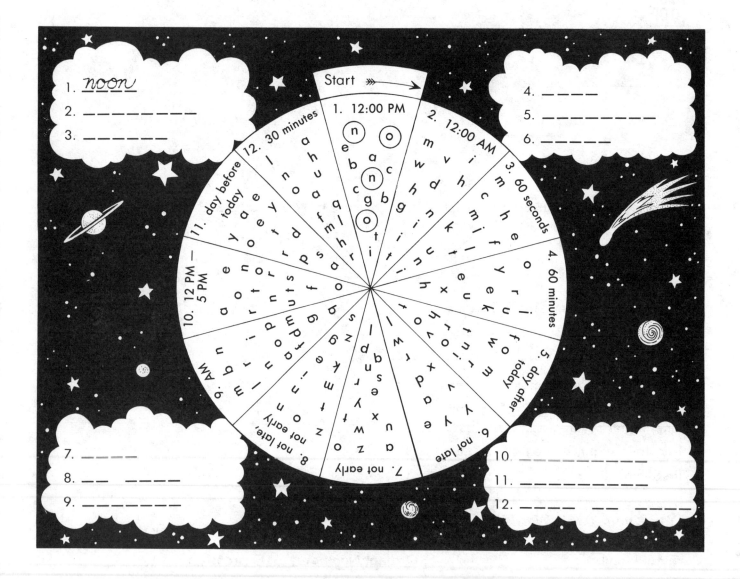

1. *noon*
2. _ _ _ _ _ _ _ _
3. _ _ _ _ _ _

4. _ _ _ _
5. _ _ _ _ _ _ _ _
6. _ _ _ _ _

7. _ _ _ _ _
8. _ _   _ _ _ _
9. _ _ _ _ _ _ _

10. _ _ _ _ _ _ _ _
11. _ _ _ _ _ _ _ _ _
12. _ _ _ _   _ _ _ _ _

2 Match Time

Match the *clocks* and the time.

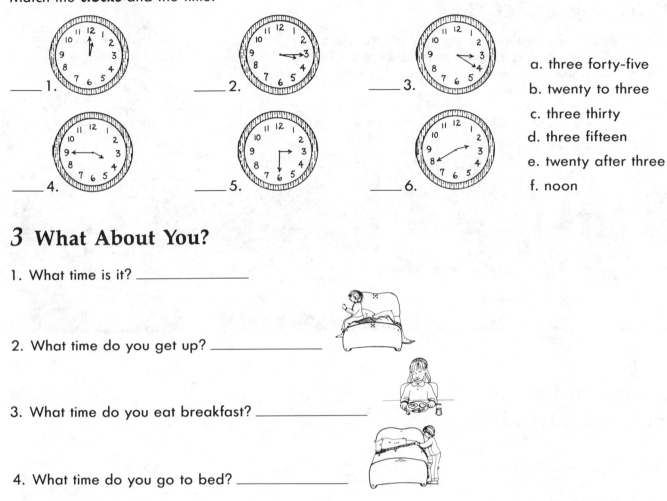

_____ 1.

_____ 2.

_____ 3.

_____ 4.

_____ 5.

_____ 6.

a. three forty-five

b. twenty to three

c. three thirty

d. three fifteen

e. twenty after three

f. noon

3 What About You?

1. What time is it? _____

2. What time do you get up? _____

3. What time do you eat breakfast? _____

4. What time do you go to bed? _____

4 Guess the Time

Read about Johnny's schedule. Then answer the question.

On Mondays Johnny meets Rosie and Artie at 6:00 P.M. Two hours *later* he packs his saxophone and goes to the Black Hat Music Club in Carson City. He is at the club a half an hour later. His concert is 30 minutes later. Johnny plays at the club for two hours. Then he goes home and arrives there a half hour later. His cat Maggie greets him in his living room. Johnny gives her milk. Fifteen minutes later, Johnny goes to bed.

Question: What time does Johnny go to bed?

a. 11:00   b. 11:30   c. 11:45   d. 12:00

Do You Know These Words?

Nouns		Adjectives	Prepositions	Expressions
afternoon	noon	early	after	eat breakfast
clock	schedule	late	before	get up
half an hour	second	later		go to bed
hour	time			on time
midnight	today			
minute	tomorrow			
morning	yesterday			

1 Keeping 🛤 of Time

Rosie and the Firefighters must be in Endsville **by** 7:30 P.M. But the **train stops** at every ⬡ .
Read their starting time at Starterup **station**. Then add the minutes on the first ⬡ to the
time and write the new time on the 🛤 . Continue **until** Endsville.

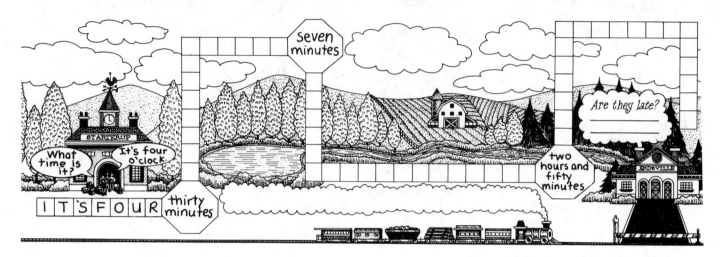

2 Time to Decide

Look at the picture. Read the statements. Then circle the correct answers.

1. Rosie and the Firefighters are (at the train station) / in the train.

2. It's summer / winter.

3. There are two / three stations in the picture.

4. The station in Starterup / Endsville has a clock.

5. It's 4:00 A.M. / 4:00 P.M.

6. It's / It isn't cloudy.

7. The train makes three / four stops before Endsville.

8. The first / third stop is a half an hour.

9. The train stops for three hours and twenty-seven minutes / two hours and thirty-seven minutes.

10. Rosie and the Firefighters are three minutes late / early.

3 Digital Watch Match

Read the times. Find the correct *digital* time. Draw a **BOX** around it.

4:15 A.M.	1:20 A.M.	12:00 P.M.	9:00 A.M.
6:45 P.M.	5:30 P.M.	7:20 P.M.	2:00 A.M.
8:00 P.M.	9:50 P.M.	6:00 A.M.	4:50 A.M.
2:30 P.M.	3:15 A.M.	1:00 P.M.	5:00 A.M.

1. It's two o'clock *sharp.*
2. It's eight o'clock *at night.*
3. It's one *in the afternoon.*
4. It's two thirty in the afternoon.
5. It's ten to ten at night.
6. It's noon.
7. It's a quarter after four *in the morning.*
8. It's five in the morning.
9. It's a quarter to seven at night.
10. It's twenty after one in the morning.

Now write all the times that are NOT in **BOXES** in words.

a. *five thirty in the afternoon.*
b. _____
c. _____

d. _____
e. _____
f. _____

4 Taking the Train

Look at the train schedule and answer the questions.

LEAVE			ARRIVE
Lincoln	Jamaica	Old Town	Homeport
12:10	12:30	12:45	1:10
1:10	1:30	1:45	2:10
2:10	_____	_____	3:00
3:30	_____	_____	4:20
4:30	_____	_____	5:20
5:10	5:30	5:45	6:10

1. What time does the 12:10 train **leave** Jamaica? ___12:30___

2. What time does it **arrive** in Homeport? _____

3. Does the 1:10 train stop **before** Homeport? _____

   If "yes," where? _____

4. Does the 2:10 train stop before Homeport? _____

   If "yes," where? _____

5. Rosie is in Jamaica. She is meeting Johnny in Old Town
   at 3:00. Which train does Rosie **take**? _____

6. Artie is meeting Rosie in Homeport at 4:00. He leaves
   Lincoln at 3:30. Is he on time? _____

7. Johnny is on the 1:10 train. How many minutes is the **trip from**
   Lincoln **to** Homeport? _____

8. Rosie is on the 2:10 train. How many minutes is her
   trip from Lincoln to Homeport? _____

Do You Know These Words?

Nouns	Verbs	Prepositions	Expressions
station	arrive	before	at night
stop	leave	by (8:00)	in the afternoon
train	stop	from. . . to	in the morning
trip	take	until	(2:00) sharp

1 Unmix and Match

Unscramble the words under each picture. Write each word on the lines on the left below.

1 ceand	2 kawl	3 snig	4 uby
5 stilen	6 wrok	7 apesk	8 thace
9 eta	10 dytus	11 aclen	12 phel

Use each word in a sentence about each picture.

1. d (a) n c e _Rosie and Artie are dancing._
2. _____ _____
3. _ (○) _ _ _____
4. _____ _____ _food._
5. _____ (○) _____ _to the radio._
6. _ (○) _ _ _____
7. _ (○) _ _ _____
8. _____ (○) _____
9. (○) _ _ _____ _ice cream._
10. _____ _____
11. (○) _ _ _ _ _____ _the kitchen._
12. _____ _____ _Artie._

Unscramble the circled letters above to spell another word. ○○○○○○○

2 What's Happening?

Look at the picture. Then read Artie's letter and complete it.

Dear Tom,

Hi! I'm in Johnny's <u>b e d r o o m</u>. Rosie is _____ the guitar and _____ a song. Johnny is _____ and _____ ice cream. Johnny's cat Maggie is on the _____. She is _____ to the music. Johnny's cousin Stuart is _____ sweaters in a _____. Phyllis is _____ him. Tomorrow we are giving a rock concert in

3 Which Word Doesn't Belong?

1. sing   speak   ~~buy~~

2. eat   walk   dance

3. eat   speak   help

4. teach   buy   study

5. listen   speak   clean

6. work   eat   teach

4 What's the Difference?

Look at the two pictures. There are seven differences. Can you find them?

Picture A

1. _Johnny is playing the saxophone._
2. _____
3. _____
4. _____
5. _____
6. _____
7. _____

Picture B

Johnny is playing the accordion.
_____
_____
_____
_____
_____
_____

5 What About You?

Answer the questions with **Yes** or **No**.

1. Are you eating? (If **yes,** WHAT are you eating?)

_____

2. Are you listening to music? (If **yes**, WHAT KIND?)

_____

3. Are the students in your class speaking? (If **yes**, WHAT LANGUAGES?)

_____

4. Are you studying? (If **yes,** WHAT?)

_____

Do You Know These Words?

Nouns	Verbs		
class	buy	practice	work
food	clean	sing	
ice cream	dance	speak	
language	eat	study	
student	help	teach	
teacher	listen	walk	

1 The Extraterrestrial

📖 This is Rosie and the Firefighters' record album. The album's name is *THE EXTRATERRESTRIAL*. Unscramble the names of the parts of the **body.**

1. rahi

2. yee

3. hade

4. sone

5. rae

6. thoum

7. ohott

8. gonute

9. knec

10. ram

11. reingf

12. cafe

13. thoacms

14. gel

15. ofto

16. dnah

Write the body parts.

1. *hair*

2. _____

3. _____

4. _____

5. _____

6. _____

7. _____

8. _____

9. _____

10. _____

11. _____

12. _____

13. _____

14. _____

15. _____

16. _____

2 What About Rosie?

Answer the questions.

How many. . .

1. eyes   2
2. tongues   _____
3. teeth   does Rosie have?   _____
4. feet   _____
5. noses   _____

3 Top Ten

These are songs on *THE EXTRATERRESTRIAL*. Circle the first letters to find the parts of the body.

THE EXTRATERRESTRIAL

SIDE 1

1. I AM A ROCK MUSICIAN   *arm*
2. EGGPLANTS ARE NOT GREEN OR RED
3. FLOWERS ARE IN COLORS EVERYDAY
4. LATE AND EARLY IN MY GARDEN
5. HELLO, ARE YOU IN YOUR ROOM?

SIDE 2

1. NINE O'CLOCK ONE SEPTEMBER, EARLY
2. HAVE A NICE BLUE DAY
3. NOW IT'S EIGHT, AND THE CAT'S IN THE KITCHEN
4. EIGHT AND THREE ARE—YES—ELEVEN
5. FALSE, OR IS IT OH SO TRUE?

4 Analogies

Complete the analogies

1. finger : hand = ____*toe*____ : foot
2. knee : leg = _____ : arm
3. fingers : ten = eyes : _____
4. mouth : sing = _____ : listen

5 What's the Sense?

Match the pictures and words.

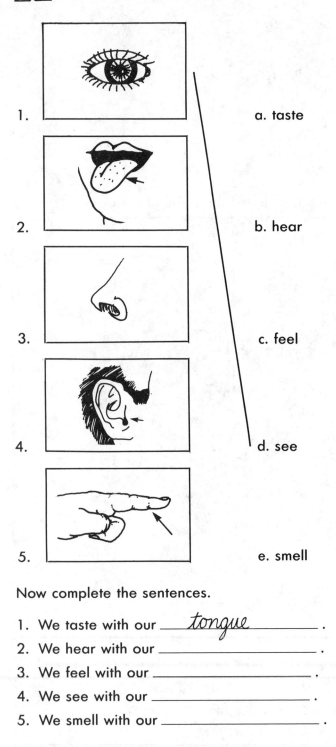

1.　　　　　　　　　　　a. taste

2.　　　　　　　　　　　b. hear

3.　　　　　　　　　　　c. feel

4.　　　　　　　　　　　d. see

5.　　　　　　　　　　　e. smell

Now complete the sentences.

1. We taste with our _____ *tongue* _____ .
2. We hear with our _____ .
3. We feel with our _____ .
4. We see with our _____ .
5. We smell with our _____ .

Do You Know These Words?

Nouns				Verbs	Expression
arm	finger	knee	toe	feel	How many?
ear	foot (feet)	leg	tongue	hear	
elbow	hair	mouth	tooth (teeth)	see	
eye	hand	nose		smell	
face	head	stomach		taste	

1 Food Memory Game

Fold this page back along the fold line (fold ⟵⟶). Follow the directions for Part 1.

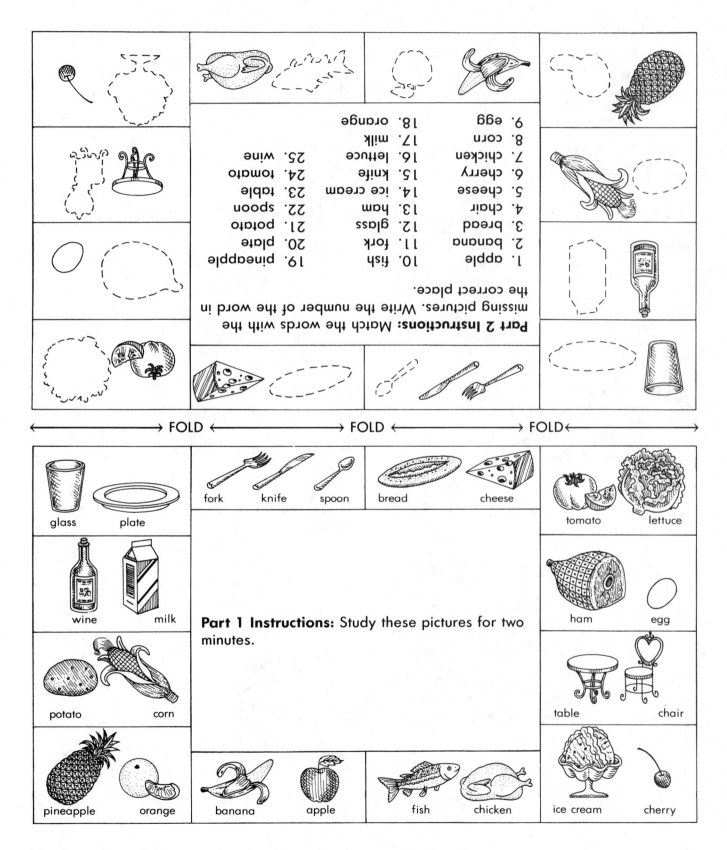

Part 2 Instructions: Match the words with the missing pictures. Write the number of the word in the correct place.

1. apple	10. fish	19. pineapple
2. banana	11. fork	20. plate
3. bread	12. glass	21. potato
4. chair	13. ham	22. spoon
5. cheese	14. ice cream	23. table
6. cherry	15. knife	24. tomato
7. chicken	16. lettuce	25. wine
8. corn	17. milk	
9. egg	18. orange	

⟶ FOLD ⟵   ⟶ FOLD ⟵   ⟶ FOLD⟵

glass   plate

fork   knife   spoon   bread   cheese

tomato   lettuce

wine   milk

Part 1 Instructions: Study these pictures for two minutes.

ham   egg

potato   corn

table   chair

pineapple   orange   banana   apple   fish   chicken   ice cream   cherry

Now turn the page over to Part 2. Follow the directions for Part 2.

2 Animal, Vegetable or Mineral?

Look at the pictures in the Food Memory Game on page 31. Write the words in the correct column.

Animal	Vegetable	Mineral
cheese	*tomato*	*glass*

3 Dinah's Diner

Rosie is eating **lunch** at Dinah's Diner. Look at Rosie's food. Then look at the **menu**. How much will Rosie's **check** be? Complete it.

LUNCH

Sandwiches

cheese 1.95
ham 2.75
hamburger 2.65
chicken 3.75
fish....................................4.75

Side Orders

lettuce and tomato salad..1.25
potato 1.05
corn 85

Desserts

ice cream 1.25
cake..................................1.75

Beverages

milk 55
coffee / tea 50

```
┌─────────────────────────────────┐
│           CHECK                 │
│  ─────────────────              │
│  hamburger          $2.65       │
│  ─────────────    ──────────    │
│  ─────────────    ──────────    │
│  ─────────────    ──────────    │
│  ─────────────    ──────────    │
│  ─────────────    ──────────    │
│  ─────────────    ──────────    │
│  ─────────────    ──────────    │
│           Total    $            │
└─────────────────────────────────┘
```

4 What About You?

1. Do you eat chicken? _____
2. Do you like ice cream? If yes, what **flavor** (**chocolate,**
   vanilla, strawberry, . . .)? _____
3. What's your favorite vegetable? _____
4. What's your favorite dessert? _____
5. What's your favorite beverage? _____
6. You have $5.50. Look at the menu in Dinah's Diner.
   What will you eat? _____

5 Which Word Doesn't Belong?

1. milk wine ~~bread~~   6. potato corn pineapple

2. knife plate fork   7. ham chicken cherry

3. apple orange egg   8. ice cream lettuce tomato

4. table glass chair   9. corn banana fish

5. cheese milk banana   10. glass plate bread

Do You Know These Words?

Nouns

animal	cheese	fish	lettuce	salad	total
apple	cherry	food	lunch	sandwich	vanilla
banana	chicken	fork	menu	side order	vegetable
beverage	chocolate	glass	mineral	spoon	wine
bread	coffee	ham	orange	strawberry	
cake	corn	hamburger	pineapple	table	
chair	dessert	ice cream	plate	tea	
check	egg	knife	potato	tomato	

1 "A" Search

Rosie and the Firefighters are at the **airport**. There are 18 items that begin with the letter A. What are they?

airport

2 Airport Signs

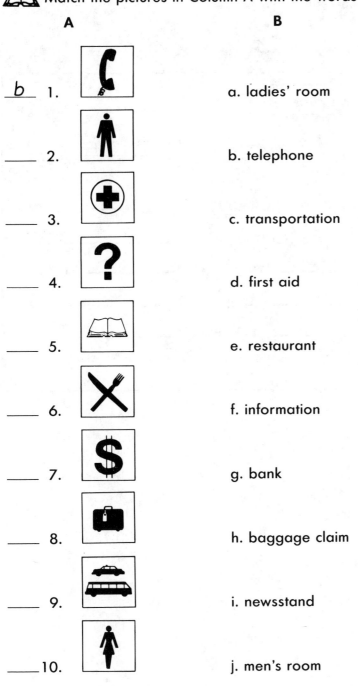 Match the pictures in Column A with the words in Column B.

A		B
_b_ 1.		a. ladies' room
___ 2.		b. telephone
___ 3.		c. transportation
___ 4.		d. first aid
___ 5.		e. restaurant
___ 6.		f. information
___ 7.		g. bank
___ 8.		h. baggage claim
___ 9.		i. newsstand
___10.		j. men's room

3 Where Is Rosie Going?

Read the conversation. Then look at the **map.**
Where is Rosie going?

ROSIE: Excuse me. Where is the

_____, please?

AGENT: Walk **straight ahead.** Then **turn right**.
The telephones are there. The

_____ is **to the left of**

the telephones.

ROSIE: Thank you.

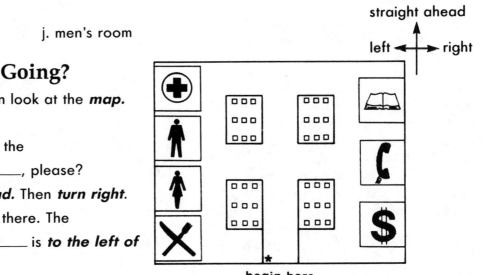

begin here

4 Destinations

Look at the **departure board.** Then complete the sentences.

```
┌─────────────────────────────────────────────────────────────┐
│                      │ Rock Airlines │                       │
│                                                               │
│  FLIGHT ════════════ DEPARTING FOR ═══════ TIME ═══════ GATE  │
│                                                               │
│  821 ─────────────── Chicago ──────────── 8:30 AM ──────── 5A │
│                                                               │
│  396 ─────────────── Boston ───────────── 10:00 AM ─────── 12A│
│                                                               │
│  482 ─────────────── Miami ────────────── 12:05 PM ─────── 5B │
│                                                               │
│  601 ─────────────── Los Angeles ──────── 1:15 PM ──────── 6A │
│                                                               │
│  276 ─────────────── Dallas ───────────── 2:35 PM ──────── 7B │
└─────────────────────────────────────────────────────────────┘
```

1. Flight 821 is going to _____*Chicago*_____ .

2. The plane to _____ is at Gate 5B.

3. The flight to _____ leaves at 10:00 A.M.

4. Flight 601 is going to _____ .

5. The plane to _____ is at Gate 7B.

Do You Know These Words?

Nouns		Verbs	Directions	Expression
airplane (plane)	gate	go	left	Excuse me.
airport	information	leave	right	
baggage	ladies' room		straight ahead	
baggage claim	map		to the left of	
bank	men's room			
city	newsstand			
departure board	restaurant			
first aid	telephone			
flight	transportation			

1 Snack Time 1 (An Irregular Meal)

Each fish eats all the letters of its irregular past tense verb. Take a pencil. Fill in the correct circles.
Begin with fish #1. You have five minutes. Ready? Begin!

2 Match the Catch 1!

Each fish has a name. Match the fish with the fish of the same number in SNACK TIME 1. Write a
sentence with the name and the irregular past tense form of the verb.

1. *Rosie saw her aunt on Monday.*
2. _____
3. _____
4. _____
5. _____
6. _____
7. _____

3 Crossword Puzzle

Complete the sentences with past tense verbs. Then write them in the puzzle.

ACROSS

2. The fish _swam_ in the bathtub.
5. Maggie _____ the fish.
8. Rosie _____ Johnny's grandmother.
9. Maggie _____ some milk.

DOWN

1. They _____ a clock at the station.
3. Johnny _____ his aunt at 5:00.
4. They _____ the 3:00 train.
6. Artie _____ a banana.
7. Rosie _____ an early class.

Do You Know These Words?

Verbs

catch / caught	find / found	know / knew	swim / swam
drink / drank	have / had	meet / met	take / took
eat / ate	hold / held	see / saw	think / thought

1 Snack Time 2!

Each fish eats all the letters of its irregular past tense verb. Take a pencil. Fill in the correct circles. Begin with fish #1. You have four minutes. Ready? Begin!

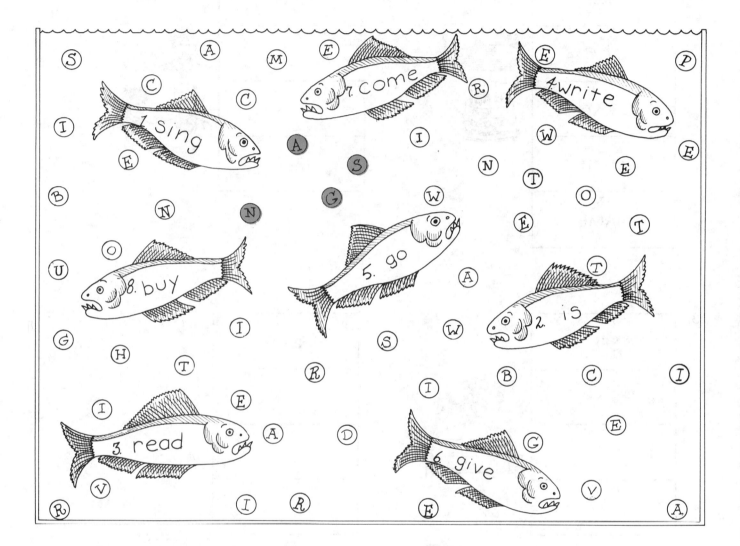

2 Match the Catch 2!

Each fish has a name. Match the fish with the fish of the same number in SNACK TIME 2. Write a sentence with the name and irregular past tense form of the verb.

1. *Rosie sang a song.*
2. _____
3. _____
4. _____
5. _____
6. _____
7. _____

3 Word Ladders

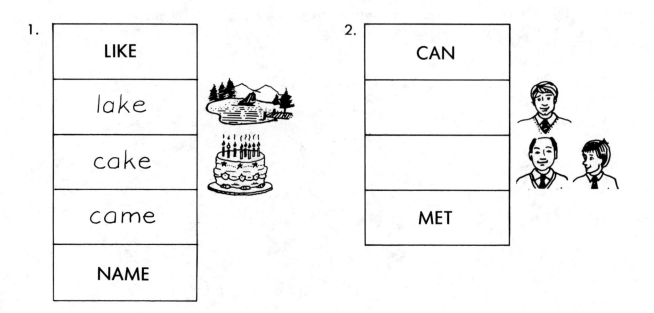 Complete these word ladders. Start with the word on top. Change one letter at a time.

1.

LIKE
lake
cake
came
NAME

2.

CAN
MET

3.

SEE
ROD

4.

READ
DEER

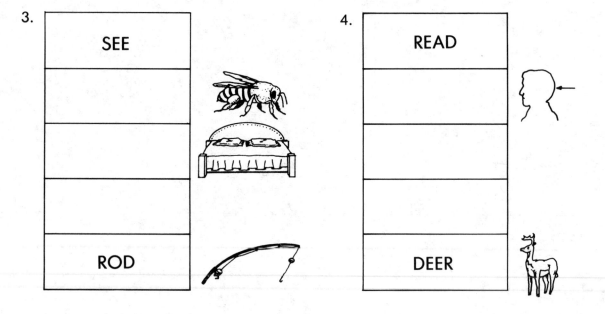

___

Do You Know These Words?

Verbs

buy / bought	give / gave	like / liked	read / read
come / came	go / went	live / lived	see / saw
cut / cut	hear / heard	love / loved	sing / sang
eat / ate	is / was	meet / met	write / wrote

1 What's My J ___ B?

📖 Look at the pictures. Then write the name of the *job.* Use the letters A, E, I, O and U.

1. artist
2. d_nt_st
3. d_ct_r
4. n_rs_
5. f_r_f_ght_r
6. p_l_t
7. b_tch_r
8. b_k_r
9. f_rm_r
10. _str_n__t
11. v_t_r_n_r__n
12. g_rd_n_r
13. m_ch_n_c
14. t__ch_r
15. _l_ctr_c__n
16. c_rp_nt_r
17. p__n_st
18. m_s_c__n

2 Picture This

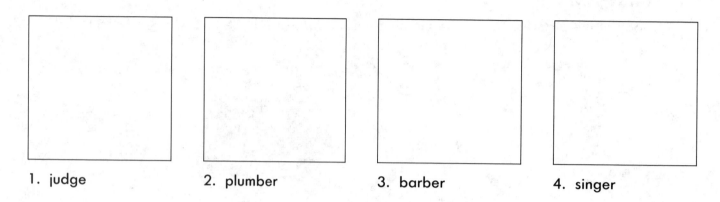 Draw a symbol for these jobs. Show your classmates.

1. judge   2. plumber   3. barber   4. singer

3 Job Search

There are 10 jobs in this box. The words go ⟶ and ↓. Can you find them?

```
T E A C H E R  D O L
A L R F A R M E R Y
D E T S E A D N O T
S C I P I L O T E N
A T S O J A M I S N
H R T L U S Y S O U
A I R Y D O C T O R
T C O O G A S H I S
M I K S E A R T O E
B A K E R T O M M Y
A N M A R N I E S U
```

1. _teacher_
2. _____
3. _____
4. _____
5. _____
6. _____
7. _____
8. _____
9. _____
10. _____

4 Which Word Doesn't Belong?

1. doctor ~~mechanic~~ dentist   4. pilot astronaut artist

2. baker butcher gardener   5. carpenter musician plumber

3. singer pianist astronaut

Do You Know These Words?

Nouns

artist	butcher	electrician	job	nurse	singer
astronaut	carpenter	farmer	judge	pianist	teacher
baker	dentist	firefighter	mechanic	pilot	veterinarian (vet)
barber	doctor	gardener	musician	plumber	

1 Characteristics

This is a game for two. Flip a coin. If it's  , say the adjective for the picture in the box. If it's  , say the opposite. Use the words in the box. You get one point for each correct answer. The person with the most points wins.

EXAMPLE:

(adjective) **hot**

(opposite adjective) **cold**

Adjectives

angry	empty	hot	rich	thin
beautiful	energetic	lazy	sad	tired
big	fat	little	short	ugly
calm	full	loving	sick	weak
cold	happy	old	strong	well
diligent	hateful	poor	tall	young

2 Opposites Attract

Unscramble the words in Column A. Then write them next to their opposites in Column B.

A

1. ullf _____
2. pahyp _____
3. unyog _____
4. rute _____
5. gib ___*full*___
6. hirc _____
7. aft _____
8. kwea _____
9. thros _____
10. lufbietua _____

B

a. thin
b. old
c. poor
d. tall
e. empty
f. strong
g. sad
h. false
i. ugly
j. little

3 Picture This

Cross out the words that DO NOT belong.

1.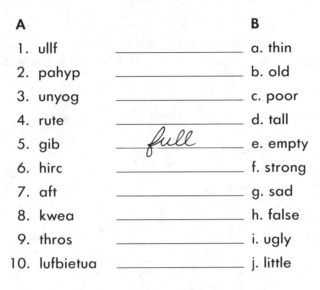

~~sad~~
young
beautiful
~~fat~~

2.

tired
old
energetic
diligent

3.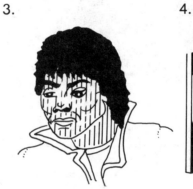

thin
calm
angry
happy

4.

black
energetic
loving
big

Now read the words. Draw a picture.

5.

~~empty~~
beautiful
old
small

4 A Love Song

Rosie and the Firefighters sing this song. Complete it with the words in the box. Every two lines rhyme. For example, **hat** rhymes with **cat**.

bad	speak
blue	strong
~~crazy~~	true
lazy	weak
sad	wrong
song	

People say I'm ___*crazy*___ .
1

People say I'm _____ ,
2

But they are _____ .
3

Come listen to my _____ .
4

I hear you _____ .
5

And I feel _____ .
6

When you are _____ ,
7

I feel so _____ .
8

My love is _____ .
9

Her eyes are _____ .
10

I feel so _____ .
11

Come hear my _____ .
12

1 Sports Tic-Tac-Toe

📖 **Rules:** One player is X, and one player is O.

Player X: Pick a **sport.** Answer the question. If the answer is right, put an X in the small box ☒ .

Player O: Pick a sport. Answer the question. If the answer is right, put an O in the small box ⬜Ⓞ .
The first player to get all the answers right horizontally (⟷), vertically (↕), or diagonally (↗ ↘)
is the **winner.**

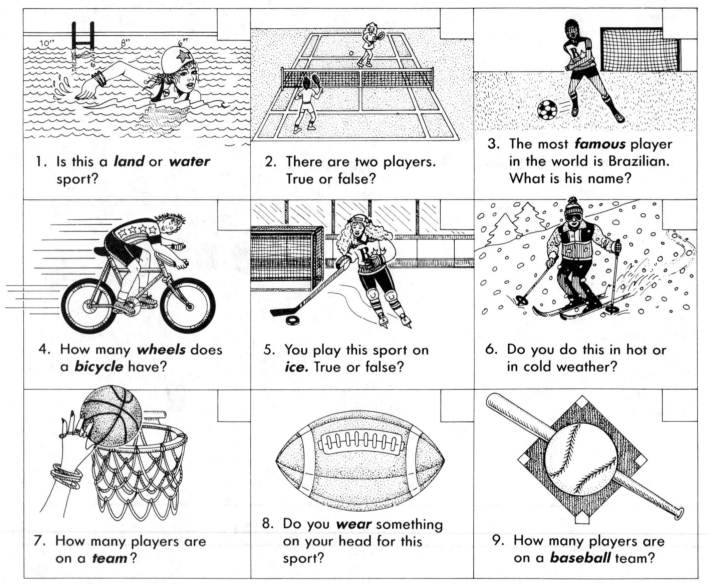

1. Is this a **land** or **water** sport?

2. There are two players. True or false?

3. The most **famous** player in the world is Brazilian. What is his name?

4. How many **wheels** does a **bicycle** have?

5. You play this sport on **ice.** True or false?

6. Do you do this in hot or in cold weather?

7. How many players are on a **team**?

8. Do you **wear** something on your head for this sport?

9. How many players are on a **baseball** team?

2 Sports Fill-In

📖 Complete the sports. Fill in the blanks with *A, E, I, O, U* or *Y.*

1. sw _i_ mm _i_ ng

2. sk __ __ ng

3. b __ c __ cl __ ng

4. h __ ck __ __

3 Have a Ball!

Complete the puzzle. Write the name of the sport that uses these items.

ACROSS

1.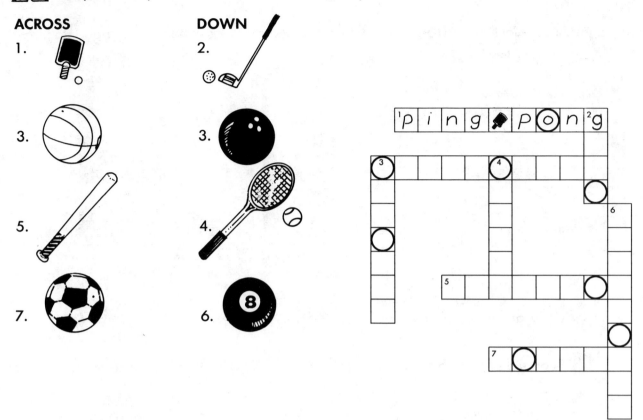
3.
5.
7.

DOWN

2.
3.
4.
6.

Unscramble the letters in the circles.

4 What About You?

1. What sports do you like? _____
2. What sports don't you like? _____
3. What sports do you play? _____
4. What sports do you watch? _____

_____

Do You Know These Words?

Nouns				Verb	Adjective
ball	football	player	tennis	wear	famous
baseball	golf	skiing	water		
basketball	hockey	soccer	wheel		
bicycle	ice	sports	winner		
billiards	land	swimming			
bowling	Ping-Pong	team			

1 Where Does It Go?

Johnny has a job in an **electronics store.** Help Johnny put the new **equipment** in the right place.

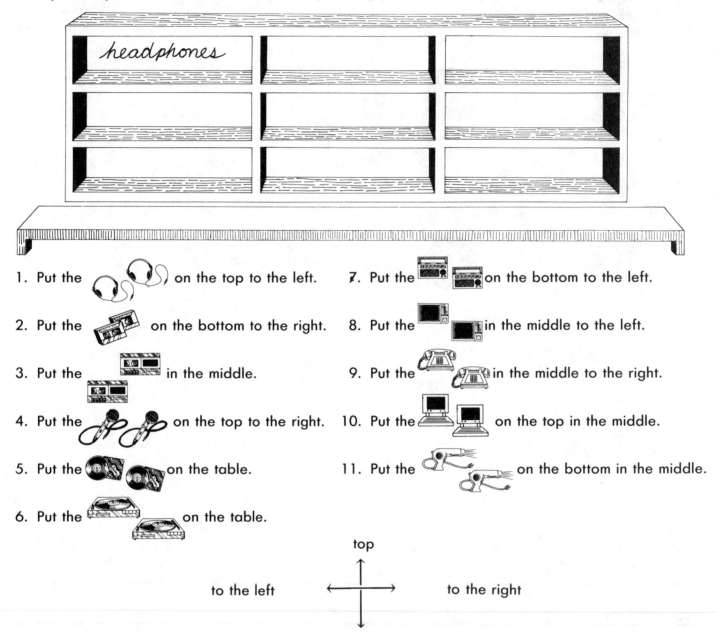

1. Put the ⬛ on the top to the left.

2. Put the ⬛ on the bottom to the right.

3. Put the ⬛ in the middle.

4. Put the ⬛ on the top to the right.

5. Put the ⬛ on the table.

6. Put the ⬛ on the table.

7. Put the ⬛ on the bottom to the left.

8. Put the ⬛ in the middle to the left.

9. Put the ⬛ in the middle to the right.

10. Put the ⬛ on the top in the middle.

11. Put the ⬛ on the bottom in the middle.

top

to the left ←——→ to the right

bottom

Equipment

cassettes
computers
headphones
hair dryers
microphones
radios

records
stereos
tape recorders
telephones
televisions

2 Word Find

Look at Rosie's room. Then look at the box. There are 16 items from Rosie's room in the box. The words go ←, →, ↑, ↓, ↘ and ↗. Find the words and put a ✓ in the picture of Rosie's room. You know all the words!

```
A R S L W O C B E A T O M Y
E M A R A L H A D V O C T E
M L P R O D A D P I P L J O
A B R U N N I N G S H O E N
T D E P F K R B L E W C E G
N I M L H C N O P R S K P S
A N E I T O I B L O U S E L
L E N N O S Z O W Y L D O I
P I C T U R E E T M R R T C
I G W A P P L E S K O O B N
N W S A T U B S V W O C X E
L I K E L G A S R I L E C P
S M I T H L T M A G F R I B
H E A D P H O N E S Y B E C
```

1. _____books_____
2. _____
3. _____
4. _____
5. _____
6. _____
7. _____
8. _____
9. _____
10. _____
11. _____
12. _____
13. _____
14. _____
15. _____
16. _____

UNIT 1

1 Meet and Greet the Stars   True or False?
1. False. Her name is Rosie.   2. True.   3. False. She plays the guitar.   4. False. Johnny plays the saxophone.   5. False. There are six drums.   6. False. Artie plays the drums.   7. True.

3 Mix and Match
1. e   2. a   3. c   4. b   5. d

4 Tune Up
Across: 3. cymbals   5. guitar   6. drum
Down: 1. accordion   2. note   4. saxophone

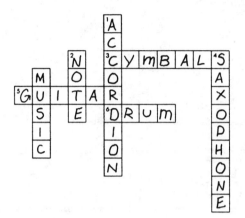

5 A Letter from Rosie
1. Hi   2. group   3. musicians   4. travel   5. concerts   6. sing   7. instrument   8. instrument   9. kind

UNIT 2

1 Colorama
1. red   2. orange   3. purple   4. yellow   5. pink   6. green   7. blue   8. white   9. gray   10. black

2 Splash!
1. red + yellow = orange   2. blue + red = purple   3. blue + yellow = green   4. white + red = pink
5. white + black = gray

3 The Rhyming Room
1. The light is white.   2. The backpack is black.   3. The bed is red.   4. The sink is pink.   5. The shoe is blue.
6. The tray is gray.

4 Picture Puzzle
1. ~~king~~free = ngree = green   2. ~~pail~~pen~~drsup~~ = ppelru = purple   3. ~~chot~~wtie = hwtie = white
Artie's sweater is green, purple and white.

UNIT 3

2 Family Find
1.–12. grandmother, cat, mother, dog, uncle, bird,
        grandfather, sister, father, aunt, cousin, brother

3 Family Match
1. g   2. c   3. i   4. b   5. e   6. d   7. f   8. a   9. h   10. h

UNIT 4

1 Where Are They?
1. garden 2. kitchen 3. dining room 4. bedroom 5. garage 6. living room 7. bathroom 8. kitchen 9. tree

2 True or False?
1. False. Phyllis is on the bedroom floor. 2. True. 3. False. The cat is on the bathtub. 4. False. There is fruit on the table in the living room. 5. False. The refrigerator is white. 6. False. There is a couch in the living room. 7. True. 8. False. There is a toilet in the bathroom. 9. False. There are flowers in the garden. 10. True.

3 Secret Code
1 = n	2 = a	3 = h	4 = l	5 = y	6 = t	7 = j
8 = m	9 = o	10 = e	11 = r	12 = k	13 = g	14 = d

Where is Mark? In the garden.

UNIT 5

1 Late for a Concert
Unscrambled words: Things in Rosie's suitcase coat, blouse, shirt, wallet, jacket, money, skirt, pants, shoes, running shoes, boots, sweater, dress
Things not in Rosie's suitcase sunglasses, bag, socks, camera, belt, records, cap, gloves, radio, hat, bathing suit, stereo

2 True or False?
1. False. This is Rosie's living room. 2. True. 3. True. 4. False. There is a picture of a guitar on the record album.
5. False. There are stripes on Rosie's sweater. 6. True. 7. False. There is a clock on the wall.

3 What Are They?
1. a. bathing suit b. sweater c. bag d. running shoes
2. a. blouse b. socks c. bag d. shirt

4 Which Word Doesn't Belong?
1. skirts 2. bag 3. camera 4. sunglasses 5. pants

5 Blue Shoe Rock
1. blue 2. you 3. chair 4. there 5. clock 6. rock 7. hat 8. cat 9. glove 10. love 11. shoe 12. do

UNIT 6

1 Name the Day
1. Sunday 2. Monday 3. Tuesday 4. Wednesday 5. Thursday 6. Friday 7. Saturday

2 Weather Watch
cloudy, rainy, sunny, windy
Sunday, cloudy; Monday, rainy; Tuesday, windy; Wednesday, sunny; Thursday, sunny; Friday, rainy; Saturday, rainy

3 Artie's Schedule
1. Monday 2. Chicago 3. sunny 4. Tomorrow
5. Wednesday 6. Saturday 7. Saturday 8. Sunday

52

UNIT 7

1 Name the Month
1. January 2. February 3. March 4. April 5. May 6. June 7. July 8. August 9. September 10. October 11. November 12. December

2 Season Stumper!
1. ice, water, hat, snow—winter
2. grass, rose, wind, plant—spring
3. sun, umbrella, swim, ice cream—summer
4. apple, leaf, football, fire—fall

3 Happy Birthday!
1. January 2. March 3. spring 4. July 5. May, spring

UNIT 8

1 Number Drawing
4, 13, 8, 90, 80, 70, 21, 19, 35, 46, 52, 67, 25, 18, 10, 20, 24

2 Sizing Them Up
Left to right: ninth, third, fifth, tenth, second, seventh, first, eighth, fourth, sixth

3 Rhymes
1. two 2. one 3. four 4. three 5. nine 6. ten
Unscrambled number: thirteen

4 What's Next?
1. four 2. eight 3. twelve 4. seven 5. sixty 6. six 7. thirty-two 8. seventh

UNIT 9

1 A Clockwise Game
1. noon 2. midnight 3. minute 4. hour 5. tomorrow 6. early
7. late 8. on time 9. morning 10. afternoon 11. yesterday 12. half an hour

2 Match Time
1. f 2. d 3. e 4. a 5. c 6. b

4 Guess the Time
c. 11:45

UNIT 10

1 Keeping Track of Time
Puzzle fill-ins: It's four. / It's four thirty. / It's four thirty-seven. / It's seven twenty-seven.
Are they late? No.

2 Time to Decide
1. at the train station   2. It's summer.   3. two   4. Starterup   5. 4:00 P.M.   6. It's   7. three   8. first   9. three hours and twenty-seven minutes   10. early

3 Digital Watch Match

4:15 A.M.	1:20 A.M.	12:00 P.M.	9:00 A.M.
6:45 P.M.	5:30 P.M.	7:20 P.M.	2:00 A.M.
8:00 P.M.	9:50 P.M.	6:00 A.M.	4:50 A.M.
2:30 P.M.	3:15 A.M.	1:00 P.M.	5:00 A.M.

Times not in boxes: a. five thirty in the afternoon   b. three fifteen in the morning   c. seven twenty at night   d. six in the morning *or* six o'clock sharp   e. nine in the morning *or* nine o'clock sharp   f. four fifty in the morning *or* ten to five

4 Taking the Train
1. 12:30   2. 1:10   3. Yes. Jamaica and Old Town.   4. No.   5. 1:30   6. No.   7. 60   8. 50

UNIT 11

1 Unmix and Match
Some possible sentences:
1. dance: Rosie and Artie are dancing.   2. walk: Johnny is walking.   3. sing: Rosie is singing.   4. buy: Johnny and Artie are buying food.   5. listen: Johnny is listening to the radio.   6. work: Rosie is working.   7. speak: Artie is speaking.
8. teach: The man is teaching.   9. eat: Rosie is eating ice cream.   10. study: Artie is studying.   11. clean: Johnny is cleaning the kitchen.   12. help: Rosie is helping Artie.
Unscrambled word: practice

2 What's Happening?
1. bedroom   2. playing   3. singing   4. dancing   5. eating   6. bed   7. listening   8. packing / putting   9. suitcase   10. helping

3 Which Word Doesn't Belong?
1. buy   2. eat   3. help   4. buy   5. clean   6. eat

4 What's the Difference?
1. Johnny is playing the saxophone. Johnny is playing the accordion.   2. Rosie is studying English. Rosie is studying music.   3. Rosie is eating a banana. Rosie is eating a carrot.   4. Artie is speaking English. Artie is speaking Spanish. *or* Artie isn't speaking English.   5. (In the picture on the wall) Rosie is singing. (In the picture on the wall) Rosie is dancing.
6. The cat is black. The cat is white.   7. The cat is sleeping. The cat is listening to the stereo *or* to a record.

UNIT 12

1 The Extraterrestrial
1. hair   2. eye   3. head   4. nose   5. ear   6. mouth   7. tooth   8. tongue   9. neck   10. arm   11. finger   12. face   13. stomach   14. leg   15. foot   16. hand

2 What about Rosie?
1. 2   2. 1   3. 32   4. 2   5. 1

3 Top Ten
Side 1: 1. arm   2. ear   3. face   4. leg   5. hair
Side 2: 1. nose   2. hand   3. neck   4. eye   5. foot

4 Analogies
1. toe   2. elbow   3. two   4. ear

5 What's the Sense?
1. d   2. a   3. e   4. b   5. c
1. tongue   2. ears   3. fingers   4. eyes   5. nose

UNIT 13
2 Animal, Vegetable or Mineral?
Animal: cheese, ham, egg, ice cream, fish, chicken, milk
Vegetable: tomato, bread, lettuce, cherry, apple, banana, orange, pineapple, potato, corn, wine
Mineral: glass, plate, fork, knife, spoon, table, chair

3 Dinah's Diner
hamburger	$2.65
potato	1.05
salad	1.25
tea	.50
cake	1.75
Total:	$7.20

5 Which Word Doesn't Belong?
1. bread   2. plate   3. egg   4. glass   5. banana   6. pineapple   7. cherry   8. ice cream   9. fish   10. bread

UNIT 14
1 "A" Search

accordion	alarm clock	armadillo
acrobat	album	arrow
actor	ambulance	artist
actress	anchor	astronaut
airplane	antenna	athlete
airport	apple	autograph

2 Airport Signs
1. b   2. j   3. d   4. f   5. i   6. e   7. g   8. h   9. c   10. a

3 Where Is Rosie Going?
the newsstand

4 Destinations
1. Chicago   2. Miami   3. Boston   4. Los Angeles   5. Dallas

UNIT 15
1 Snack Time 1!
1. saw   2. met   3. held   4. took   5. had   6. drank   7. caught   8. ate   9. found   10. swam   11. knew   12. thought

2 Match the Catch 1!
1. Rosie saw...   2. Artie met...   3. Kate held...   4. Mark took...   5. I had...   6. Johnny drank...
7. Phyllis caught...

3 Crossword Puzzle
Across: 2. swam   5. caught   8. knew   9. drank
Down: 1. saw   3. met   4. took   6. ate   7. had

UNIT 16

1 Snack Time 2!
1. sang 2. was 3. read 4. wrote 5. went 6. gave 7. came 8. bought

2 Match the Catch 2!
1. Rosie sang. . . 2. Kate was. . . 3. I read. . . 4. Mark wrote. . . 5. Johnny went. . . 6. Artie gave. . .
7. Phyllis came. . .

3 Word Ladders
1. like, lake, cake, came, name 2. can, man, men, met 3. see, bee, bed, red, rod 4. read, head, hear, dear, deer

UNIT 17

1 What's My J__B?
1. artist 2. dentist 3. doctor 4. nurse 5. firefighter 6. pilot 7. butcher 8. baker 9. farmer 10. astronaut
11. veterinarian 12. gardener 13. mechanic 14. teacher 15. electrician 16. carpenter 17. pianist 18. musician

3 Job Search
1.–10. teacher, farmer, pilot, doctor, baker, electrician, artist, judge, dentist, nurse

```
T E A C H E R D O L
A L R F A R M E R Y
D E T S E A D N O T
S C I P I L O T E N
A T S O J A M I S N
H R T L U S Y S O U
A I R Y D O C T O R
T C O O G A S H I S
M I K S E A R T O E
B A K E R T O M M Y
A N M A R N I E S U
```

4 Which Word Doesn't Belong?
1. mechanic 2. gardener 3. astronaut 4. artist 5. musician

UNIT 18

1 Characteristics
1. happy/sad 2. sick/well 3. angry/calm *or* happy 4. energetic/tired 5. full/empty 6. tall/short 7. loving/hateful
8. tired/energetic *or* lazy/diligent 9. beautiful/ugly 10. fat/thin 11. little/big 12. old/young 13. poor/rich
14. diligent/lazy 15. strong/weak

2 Opposites Attract
1. full, e 2. happy, g 3. young, b 4. true, h 5. big, j 6. rich, c 7. fat, a 8. weak, f 9. short, d 10. beautiful, i

3 Picture This

1. ~~sad~~	2. sleepy	3. thin	4. black
young	~~old~~	~~calm~~	~~energetic~~
beautiful	~~energetic~~	angry	loving
~~fat~~	~~diligent~~	~~happy~~	~~big~~

4 A Love Song
1. crazy 2. lazy 3. wrong 4. song 5. speak 6. weak 7. sad *or* bad 8. bad *or* sad 9. true 10. blue
11. strong 12. song

UNIT 19

1 Sports Tic-Tac-Toe
1. A water sport. 2. True. 3. Pelé. 4. Two. 5. True. 6. In cold weather. 7. Five. 8. Yes. 9. Nine.

2 Sports Fill-In
1. swimming 2. skiing 3. bicycling 4. hockey

3 Have a Ball!
Across: 1. Ping–Pong 3. basketball 5. baseball 7. soccer
Down: 2. golf 3. bowling 4. tennis 6. billiards
Unscrambled word: football

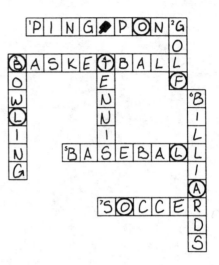

UNIT 20

1 Where Does It Go?

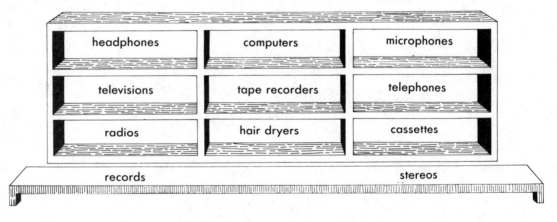

2 Word Find
1.–16. books, running shoe, blouse, picture, plant, sock, chair, floor, clock, records, pencils, cap, headphones, belt, wall, glass, table